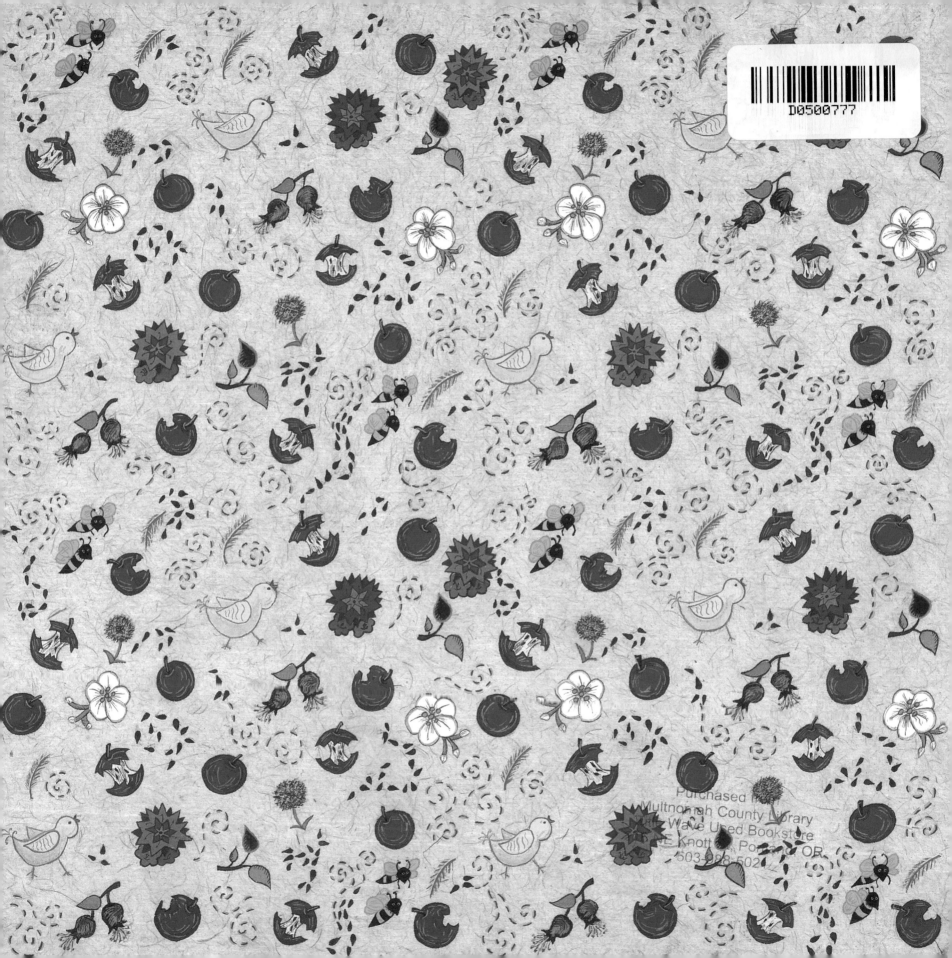

D0500777

for Lucy Rita

–H.Z.

Text copyright © 2009
by Harriet Ziefert
Illustrations copyright © 2009
by Karla Gudeon
All rights reserved / CIP Data is available.
Published in the United States 2008 by
Blue Apple Books
515 Valley Street, Maplewood
N.J. 07040
www.blueapplebooks.com

Distributed in the U.S. by
Chronicle Books
First Edition
Printed in China

ISBN: 978-1-934706-67-1

2 4 6 8 10 9 7 5 3 1

for my parents,
who raised me in a home with art,
music, books, and love

–K.G.

HARRIET ZIEFERT

One Red Apple

paintings by

KARLA GUDEON

BLUE APPLE BOOKS

One
Red 🍎
Apple

Pick

a red apple

from a tree.

Drive a ripe, red apple to market.

Buy

a sweet, red apple

at a farm

stand.

Enjoy

a crunchy,

red apple.

Delicious!

Leave

an apple core

for the birds

to eat.

Watch tiny apple seeds scatter in the wind.

See

small sprouts

peek out from

the earth.

Grow

apple tree,

grow,

year

by year . . .

Bloom

apple tree

and dress yourself

with white and

pink blossoms.

Grow

little apple, grow,

week by week,

until . . .

you're
ready
for
picking.

Thank you,
birds,
wind,
sun,
and bees.

Thank you,
earth,

for one red apple.

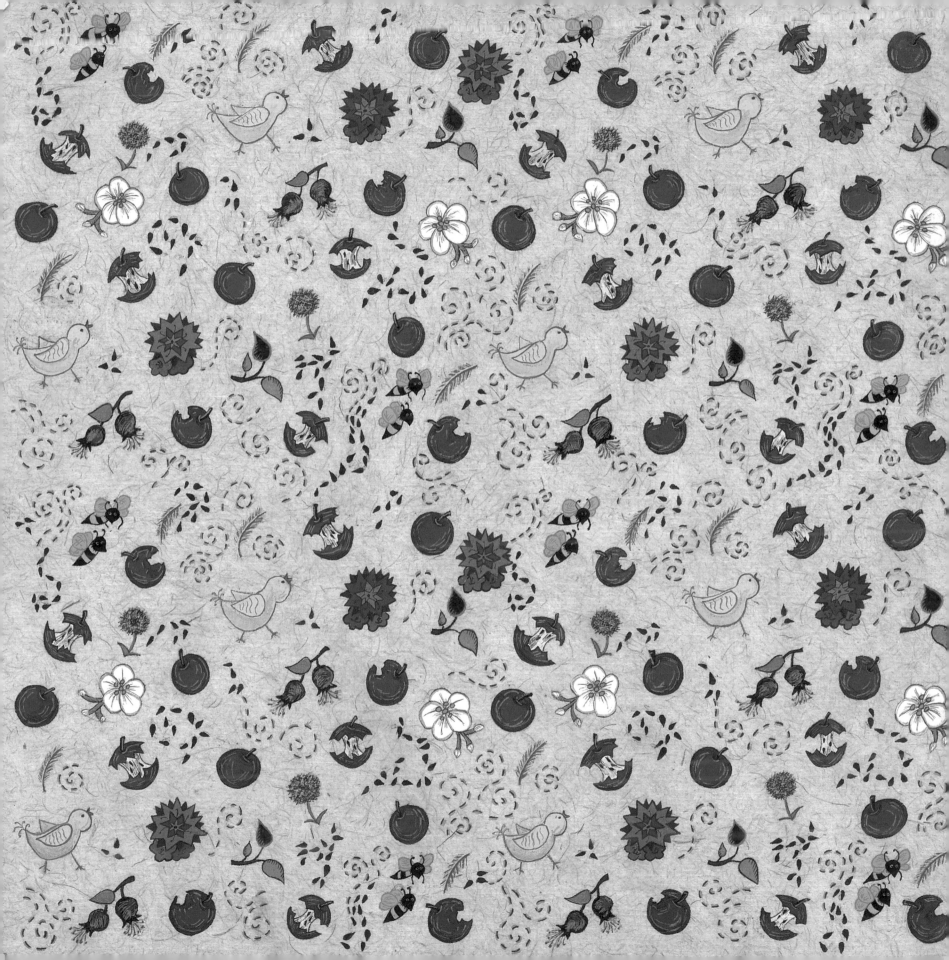